Jemmla Trindade
Jilene Coelho Ferreira

Profile of distance learning students in the Chemistry course at the Grajaú hub

Jemmla Trindade
Jilene Coelho Ferreira

Profile of distance learning students in the Chemistry course at the Grajaú hub

Focus Distance education

ScienciaScripts

Imprint

Cover image: www.ingimage.com

This book is a translation from the original published under ISBN 978-3-330-75833-9.

Publisher:
Sciencia Scripts
is a trademark of
Dodo Books Indian Ocean Ltd. and OmniScriptum S.R.L publishing group

120 High Road, East Finchley, London, N2 9ED, United Kingdom
Str. Armeneasca 28/1, office 1, Chisinau MD-2012, Republic of Moldova, Europe
Printed at: see last page
ISBN: 978-620-8-29691-9

SUMMARY

1 INTRODUCTION

This paper, entitled PROFILE OF THE STUDENTS IN THE DISTANCE CHEMISTRY COURSE AT THE GRAJAÙ POLE, seeks to offer the reader a view of the graduates of the distance chemistry course at the Open University of Brazil - UAB - Grajaù-MA pole, offered by the Federal University of Maranhão, in which the writing produced on the beginnings of Distance Education in Brazil is presented, the international influences present in its construction, the objectives and actions present in it, artifacts and public policies that made it possible for it to become effective and develop, as well as dialogues on the relationships existing in the Pedagogical Course Projects - PPC - in order to present the layout of the Degree Courses in Chemistry in the Distance Education modality managed by the Open University of Brazil platform in the Brazilian scenario.

Chemistry is an experimental science whose effects can be seen in different ways in our daily lives. This great science is actively present in various sectors of our modernity. These include: fuels, plastics, paints, health, food, petrochemicals, dyes, adhesives, drinks, cleaning materials, etc. Knowing how to make the best use of it will bring us great benefits, such as the improvement of human comforts, a decline in the number of deaths due to the evolution of medicine.

On the contrary, based on the inadequate extraction of chemical substances from nature and with only political and economic interests in mind, without worrying about the undesirable and harmful effects, they will cause illness and death of not only aquatic life, with pollution being the main cause.

Faced with the challenges that educators are facing and taking on in the search for innovation in the teaching-learning process, one of the techniques that adds the most resources for implementing a new dynamic in the routine of relations between teachers and learners is undoubtedly the new information and communication technologies used in Distance Education (DE). With the growth of distance education in the virtual environment, various pedagogical tools have emerged with the aim of facilitating the implementation of innovative pedagogical proposals and allowing access to regular and continuing training for students and professionals who find it difficult to be included in conventional teaching processes.

In distance education, the student is the active subject of his or her knowledge-building process and the teacher works as a facilitator along the way, i.e. the student interacts with the content on different media and relies on the teacher's guidance and intervention in times of difficulty or choice of different paths.

According to Almeida (2003), although distance learning carried out through conventional means of transmission makes it difficult to establish inter-relationships between sender and receiver, process and product, and has high drop-out rates, it is widespread in all parts of the world, due to the need to cater for the growing proportion of the population seeking training (initial or continuing) in order to acquire the conditions to compete in the job market.

Vygotsky (1984) points out that during the process of building knowledge, the student must rely on the help of the teacher and other students/peers.

Higher Education Institutions (HEIs) have invested in creating and maintaining virtual learning environments (VLEs) as teaching-learning tools, with the aim of organizing and facilitating the use of simulators and other devices that value individuality, seeking to stimulate ideas, opinions and attitudes, in which students exercise their ability to learn how to learn and develop the ability to reason, in order to use these already retained and matured skills in other contexts.

The educational model, adopted for hundreds of years in universities, is proving to be inefficient in serving an audience that has limited time for face-to-face study and is inserted in a market that demands a continuous teaching-learning process.

In this new educational scenario, where technological transformations have broadened demands and facilitated access to knowledge quickly and cheaply, the appropriate use of new teaching and learning tools, especially the Internet, has become fundamental to the success of HEIs in their task of preparing new generations of professionals.

For this reason, pedagogical strategies that make use of VLE are today the most important means of integrating teachers, students and professionals.

This tool makes the distance learning process more interactive by using multimedia resources, as well as making the content available in full time.

2 HISTORY OF EAD IN BRAZIL

The growing demand for training professionals in the most diverse areas, the scarcity, the distance and the high cost involved in building and maintaining training institutions, presents society with the challenge of thinking up new ways of providing training for its members. With the help of Information and Communication Technologies (ICT), Distance Education (DE) is a possibility for resolving this demand.

Through the historical trajectory of the use of ICT for distance learning, it is possible to perceive three moments, the first centered on the use of printed materials delivered by post; the second on the use of printed materials concomitantly with radio, television and videos; and thirdly, the use of the internet, an artifact that has enabled greater mediation and interaction between subjects in distance learning courses. According to the fragment of the Pedagogical Project of the Undergraduate Chemistry Course at UFMG (2005, p. 10) on the use of the internet as a power for distance learning:

> [...] this was an important moment in the "transition from distance education to education without distance, both in terms of space/time and the democratization of quality education".

In the Brazilian context, the first steps towards distance education began at the beginning of the 20th century, through correspondence courses, a movement influenced by the experience of European and North American countries at the end of the 19th century, as highlighted in another fragment of UFMG's PPC (2005, p. 9):

In the second half of the 19th century, distance learning began to exist institutionally and alongside face-to-face learning. In 1856, Charles Toussaint and Gustav Langenscheidt set up the first language school by correspondence in Berlin. That same year, Dean William R. Harper set up the Division of Correspondence Learning in the Department of Extension at the University of Chicago. In 1874, Illinois Wesleyan University began offering correspondence courses.

In this sense, the offer of distance learning courses in Brazil through the use of printed materials delivered by mail began with the Monitor Institute and the Brazilian Universal Institute - IUB, the forerunners in offering courses in this modality, as reported in the PPC of the UECE (2012, p. 7):

In the first decades of the 20th century, the first distance learning courses were offered in Brazil by the Monitor Institute, aimed at training in electronics, and by the Brazilian Universal Institute (IUB), aimed at training at primary and secondary levels.

The second moment of Distance Education in Brazil, in which the use of printed materials concomitant with the use of radio and television in the mid-20th century became present as a way of enhancing Distance Education, became significant after the experiments carried out by the Educational Radio Service of the Ministry of Education, in order to turn radio into an artifact for educational purposes.

The third moment begins at the end of the 20th century, with the first virtual support tools becoming available in Brazil, in order to intensify interaction and mediation processes in the distance education modality, both synchronously and asynchronously.

The publication of LDB No. 9.3942 in 1996, which mentions in article 80 the role of public authorities in encouraging the development and linking of distance education programs, represented a major step forward for this modality in Brazil and through the legitimization of distance education by Decree No. 2.4943 in 1998 in article 1, a definition is obtained for this modality:

> [...] a form of teaching that enables self-learning through the mediation of systematically organized didactic resources, presented in different information media, used alone or in combination, and conveyed by the various means of communication.

The trajectory of distance education in Brazil to date, in which its expansion, advances in methodologies and means of development are becoming increasingly evident, allows us to see the potential that exists in it and demonstrates the need for more and more research to understand this modality.

Grajaù is located in the Centro Maranhense mesoregion, and together with the municipalities of Arame, Barra do Corda, Joselândia, Sitio Novo and Tuntum forms the Alto Mearim and Grajaù micro-region.

The municipality of Grajaù covers an area of 7,408 square kilometers. It is 557 km from Sâo Luis, the state capital. It is linked to Sâo Luis by the BR-226 highway and the MA-006 highway. The municipality is one of the twenty most populous in Maranhão.

The seat of the municipality is 130 meters above sea level and is bordered to the north by Arame, to the northeast by Itaipava do Grajaù, to the east by Barra do Corda, to the south by Formosa da Serra Negra, to the west by Sitio Novo and to the northwest by Amarante do Maranhâo.

According to the Brazilian Institute of Geography and Statistics, the total population of the municipality in 2015 was 67,626. Around half of the population lives in the rural area of the municipality, where they work in the agricultural production that maintains the local economy, especially rice production.

2.1 Virtual Environment

According to Sabbatini (2007), the Moodle System is a Virtual Learning Environment based on free software. The term Moodle is an acronym for Modular Object-Oriented Dynamic Learning Environment. Its development community involves hundreds of programmers around the world, programming new features and improvements under the Free Software philosophy. It has one of the largest user bases with more than 25,000 server installations, more than 360,000 courses and more than 4 million students in 155 different countries. It's a very robust system, supporting tens of thousands of students on a single installation. Interestingly, one of the largest Moodle installations has over 6,000 courses and more than 45,000 students (SABBATINI, 2007).

The Open University of England has adopted Moodle for its 200,000 students, as has the UAB - Open University of Brazil. Moodle has the largest international market share, with over 54% of all online teaching and learning support systems. It is maintained by a foundation (www.moodle.org) and a company (www.moodle.com) which respectively provide support for the development of the software and its translation into dozens of languages (SABBATINI, 2007).

As its name implies, the AVA - Virtual Learning Environment makes it possible to develop activities at a more flexible time, space and pace. It provides teachers with the possibility of creating and conducting distance learning courses, through activities that require student action, such as materials for consultation, assessment and training activities, following the teaching plan.

The fundamental structure of a VLE is focused on learning, interaction, building knowledge and developing the potential of the participants involved. It is a virtual educational space that enables the integration of multiple languages, media and activities mediated by ICTs - Information and Communication Technologies. The ideal structure of a VLE focuses on learning, interaction, the construction of knowledge and the development of the potential of the participants involved. It is a virtual educational space that enables the integration of multiple languages, media and activities mediated by ICTs - Information and Communication Technologies. VLEs can be used to develop the virtual or semi-presential teaching and learning process.

Many teachers at the Federal University of Maranhao (UFMA) already use VLE for part of their face-to-face courses. Ordinance N04059 of 10 December 2004 authorizes the introduction of semi-presential courses for up to 20% of the total workload of recognized higher education courses. For example, a teacher and/or tutor can provide materials, texts, videos and audios, as well as activities. Students access these resources from anywhere they have Internet access, exchange ideas, materials, information, respond to activities, forums, etc.

Thus, it allows activities to be proposed that promote these actions and possibilities, but requires us to free ourselves from the centralized model privileged by the transmission of knowledge, evolving towards a shared process in which the teacher acts, more than in the classroom, as a member of the group, leaving the community to lead the activities of intervention, accompaniment and construction of knowledge.

In the Virtual Learning Environment, technological mediation becomes paramount in the process of building relationships. Palloff and Prat (2002), in a report on their work, understand that the relationships created in a virtual educational space can even be more emotionally intense than the inhibitions created by face-to-face communication between people. "They even believe that the communication factor - rather than the content transmitted - is what generates knowledge" (SOARES, 2003, p. 14).

Learning then becomes a shared proposition. In this way, everyone collaborates and participates effectively in individual and group growth. Learning in a collaborative environment values each person's experience and knowledge, encouraging and respecting differences and building on similarities. But how does the VLE enable the sharing of information, materials, exchange of experiences and the building of knowledge to take place satisfactorily?

According to Ribeiro; Mendonça, (2007, p. 4) VLEs:

[...] provide participants with tools to use during a course, to facilitate the sharing of study materials, hold discussions, collect and review assignments, record grades, promote interaction and other functionalities. They contribute to making the most of education and learning.

Distance learning presupposes the adoption of pedagogical strategies that encourage interactive, autonomous and collaborative student participation. And in this context it is necessary to provide the appropriate structure for planning learning using technological tools and resources, developing appropriate content for distance learning, as well as offering all the academic-pedagogical support provided by doctors, masters and specialists for this new type of teaching.

2.2 Technologies for distance learning

Sabbatini (2007) states that the VLE is made up of various tools that enable publication, interaction and evaluation. The standard tools are chat, which enables real-time, synchronous communication between teachers, tutors and students.

To take part in a chat, students must log on at a date and time set by the teacher and/or tutor, who has previously scheduled the chat session, where debates, discussions, questions can take place, among other possibilities. It can be useful as a space for clarifying doubts or for a chat with a guest, for example. The interesting thing about this tool is that the chat logs are available for later reference, i.e. they are recorded. When opening a chat, the following should always be noted:

- Communication network infrastructure and VLE hosting server;
- Feasibility of keeping fixed hours for everyone;
- Number of participants per moderator or teacher;
- The need for a moderator to select the most important issues and facilitate the organization of the discussion;
- Mandatory participation;
- Content and depth;
- Characteristics of the group: familiarity with online activities, willingness to communicate and collaborate, good rapport between participants, among others (LEITE, 2006).

The Forum is a place where teachers, tutors and students can interact through a theme or a question on a subject in the course, allowing it to be discussed. It is a very interesting and versatile asynchronous communication tool, with the following advantages:

- Encourage more thought and research before posting;
- Make it possible to better organize the content and form of the text to be posted;
- It requires correct and clear expression of ideas;
- It allows you to delve deeper into ideas and concepts;
- It facilitates the conscious practice of different cognitive functions, such

as: observing, identifying, relating, comparing, analyzing, inferring, synthesizing, diverging, disagreeing, generalizing, etc;

- It makes it possible to record the process of building knowledge;
- It allows for more targeted mediation by the teacher (LEITE, 2006).

In the same vein as the advantages of synchronous communication, Leite (2006) also comments that forums also offer some possibilities such as:

- Space for collective reflection or text discussion;
- It can serve as a page for collaborative text construction;
- Discussion of topics related to the content, mediated by the tutors;
- It can be used as a wall where students can display their work or questions; - Case studies;
- Building work or projects.

According to Nakamura (2008) there are several types of forum, but the most common is the simple discussion forum, where there is a single topic on a single page. It is usually used to organize short discussions focused on a specific topic. According to Leite (2006) "forums allow quantitative or qualitative evaluation of each message and different evaluation criteria can be created, remembering that their success depends a lot on the type of mediation".

The Questionnaire allows you to create questions with different answer formats, such as true or false, multiple choices, values, short answers, etc. Among other things, it allows you to choose questions at random, automatically correct answers and export the data to Excel.

In many distance learning courses, content assessments are carried out using the quiz tool. You can create an activity and use the tool as a retention exercise for a particular piece of content.

There are various configurations for the questionnaire, such as authorizing the student to answer several times, applying or not penalties for trying, and/or allowing or blocking student access to the correct answers, among others (LEITE, 2006).

A task is a tool that allows students to send a file online. For example, an assignment or document prepared in Word (doc.), based on an activity proposed by the tutor and/or teacher.

They are related to the famous "homework". It can be solving a list of exercises, an article, a summary or any activity proposed by the tutor and/or teacher. Like most VLE tools, it can have a deadline, set by the teacher and/or tutor, for the task to be completed. As soon as the student has finished the work, they must upload the file to the VLE, i.e. submit the activity virtually (LEITE, 2006; NAKAMURA, 2008).

2.3 Student profile in distance learning

According to the Ministry of Education and Culture, distance education is a "form of teaching that enables self-learning, with the mediation of systematically organized teaching resources, presented in different information media, used alone or in combination, and conveyed by the various means of communication" (MEC).

There is a constant debate in the academic world about who is driven to study online. It is a given that students who study online are adults, because this type of learning, which takes place anywhere and at any time, allows them to continue working full time while also taking care of their families. "The 'typical' online student is usually described as someone who is over 25, employed, concerned about the well-being of the community, with some higher education in progress, and may be both male and female." (GILBERT, 2001, p.74).

Unlike face-to-face students, who have a whole environment at their fingertips, distance learning students have some characteristics of their own that are necessary to stimulate their perception and cognition in order to hold their attention for long periods of study. On this subject, the president of ABED (the Brazilian Distance Education Association), Frederic Michael Litto, in an interview given to Folha Online reporter Camila Marques in 2004, admitted that the modality "is not for everyone". According to him: "The student who needs the teacher by his side, demanding or praising, is not good for distance education. A student who is a bit more mature and autonomous is preferable. And who meets deadlines.

Studies show that there is a constant concern to make distance learning more and more student-centered. According to Belloni (2006 p. 39) "whether from the point of view of economic paradigms, or from the perspective of major definitions" To know who the distance learning student is, it is necessary to analyze some of the characteristics that are peculiar to them.

According to Belloni (2006):

> The fundamental characteristics of contemporary society that have the greatest impact on education are therefore greater complexity, more technology, compression of space and time relationships. Work that is more responsible, more precarious, more mobile, requiring a multi-competent, multi-skilled worker, capable of managing group situations, adapting to new situations and always ready to learn. In short, a more informed and autonomous worker.

Nowadays, people are increasingly seeking autonomy and self-learning is one of the characteristics that stands out most in their profile. Today's professionals need to be versatile and always connected to new trends, improving their learning for the sake of their work and even their personal fulfillment. Trindade, apud Belloni (1992, p. 32), defines autonomous learning as a process of teaching and learning centered on the learner, and also says that the teacher must take on the role of a resource for this learner.

It would be great if this were the profile of all distance learning students. Palloff and Pratt (2004) say that this ideal student is far from the vast majority of people who seek out this type of education. According to Renner (1995), many distance learners tend to be passive learners, "digesting packets of information and regurgitating the knowledge they have assimilated at the time of assessment".

Belloni (2006) says that the potential clientele of education is changing rapidly, tending to increase in number and diversify in terms of the specific demands of globalization and localization.

Gilbert, apud Palloff and Pratt (2004) says that:

The "typical" online student is usually described as someone who is over 25, employed, concerned about the social well-being of the community, with some higher education in progress, and can be either male or female.

It can be said that the adult distance learning student is currently in the andragogy phase. Knowles (1995) defines andragogy as "the art and science of helping adults to learn, based on the basic differences between being an adult and being a child". According to this author, adults learn for the immediate application of the activities they carry out, in order to solve problems. Young people and children learn in order to store up knowledge.

Research, however, shows that there is no defined age range for distance learning courses. Palloff and Pratt (2004 p. 23) cite a survey published by the National Center for Education Statistics (2002) which shows that:

By December 31, 1999, 65% of people under the age of 18 had joined an online course, indicating the growing popularity of virtual high school courses. Fifty-seven percent of traditional university students between the ages of 19 and 23 have also joined such courses. Fifty-six percent of people aged between 24 and 29 enrolled, and the rate of people over 30 who did the same was 63%. The statistics confirm that the number of men and women is very similar. With the exception of indigenous groups and Alaskan natives (of whom only 45% enrolled in online courses), around 60% of people of all races participate in such courses.

It is understood that the increase in demand for distance learning courses is due to the facilities that this type of teaching can offer. The use of the Internet has made this easier, since there are now no communication barriers between students and their teachers.

The general aim of this work is to investigate the profile of distance learning students, based on questionnaires and reports from students on the courses. Specific objectives: To identify the main learning difficulties in distance learning; To highlight how distance education can contribute to the teaching and learning of chemistry in distance learning; To analyze the contribution of chemistry to the development of school activities.

3 METHODOLOGICAL PROCEDURES

3.1 Research Classification

The main objective of the research was to investigate the profile of distance learning students, based on questionnaires and reports from students on chemistry courses.

This work will be based on a critical-dialectical approach, through field research, with a quantitative approach aimed at surveying the profile of distance learning chemistry students.

It is known that research is the result of restlessness, doubt, uncertainty, arising from the researcher's quest to define a problem, to discover something. According to Japiassu (1983, p. 14): "our knowledge is born in doubt and feeds on uncertainty".

The aim is to carry out a survey that guarantees the representation of data and information about the students of the Chemistry course at the Grajaù campus who entered in 2010.

3.2 Sources for Data Collection

As sources of data collection, it is necessary to use primary and secondary sources that include the observation of data collected without scientific treatment, and extracted from books, magazines, that is, information with a scientific nature.

According to Andrade (2001, p. 43):

Primary sources are made up of original texts, material that has not yet been worked on, on a given subject. Secondary sources refer to certain primary sources, i.e. they are made up of literature originating from certain primary sources and are sources of bibliographic research.

To collect primary sources, interviews were carried out with the application of questionnaires, visits and telephone calls.

3.3 Identifying the Research Sample

The starting point for this research was the Open University of Brazil (UAB) Center, located in the Trizidela neighborhood in the city of Grajaù-MA. The structure of the center consists of 4 classrooms, 1 auditorium, 3 bathrooms, a coordination room, 02 laboratories (chemistry and biology), a kitchen, a meeting room, a cafeteria and a patio. This location was chosen because of the direct contact with this educational institution.

The subjects involved in the investigation were 7 (seven) chemistry undergraduates studying via distance learning.

4 Data Collection Instruments

The instrument used to collect the data was an open and closed questionnaire addressed to 07 (seven) academics studying in distance education, with 17 direct questions presented in the appendix.

A questionnaire is a research tool designed to gather information, usually based on the survey of a representative group of the population being studied. This is done by asking a series of questions covering a topic of interest to the researchers, with no direct interaction between the researchers and the respondents.

A questionnaire is extremely useful when a researcher wants to gather information on a particular topic. Thus, by applying a questionnaire to a target group of, for example, academics, it is possible to gather information that will allow us to better understand their shortcomings and improve teaching methodologies, thus being able to individualize teaching when necessary.

5 RESULTS AND DISCUSSION

5.1 Presentation of quantitative data

The way we worked with the data obtained in the survey, especially the numerical data from the questionnaires, was what we call descriptive statistics, which can be defined as the part of statistics that aims to describe and evaluate a certain group, without inferring or drawing conclusions about a larger group.

Therefore, we would like to make it clear that the aim of this study was to analyze the profile of students on the UFMA's Chemistry course in Grajaù in the distance education modality in 2010, without pretending that the analysis and discussion of the results obtained were a reality for other courses in the country. We chose to present the numerical data using simple tables and graphs. As the number of participants was a total of 07 interviewees for the questionnaire presented in Appendix 1.

Of the thirty-three (33) students enrolled in the chemistry course, only eight (08) have finished the course and of these, seven answered the questionnaire.

Figure 1 shows that the 18 to 20 age group and the 40 to 50 age group account for 0% of those interviewed. That between 30 and 40 years corresponds to 86% of those interviewed and 14% is in the 20 to 30 age group.

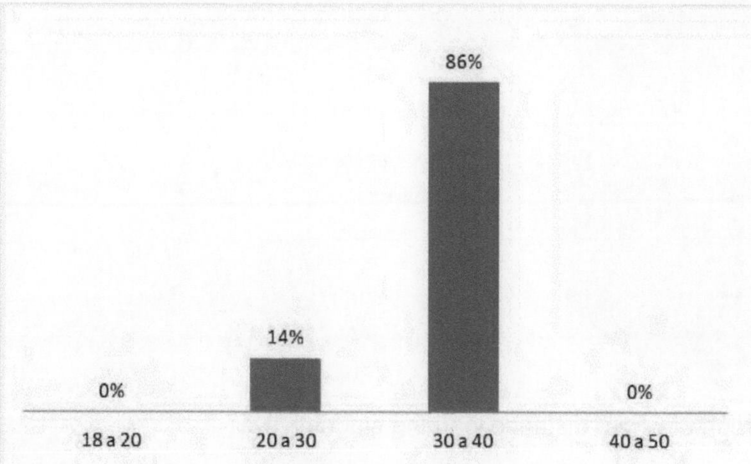

Figura 1: Graph of the age group of distance learning students

According to the 2014-2015 EAD.Br Census by the Brazilian Distance Education Association (ABED) for distance learning courses, the age group of most students is between 30 and 40 years old, fully agreeing with the results found.

It was found that 14% of the students live in rural areas. Another 14% live in other neighboring towns and the majority of students (72%) live in urban areas, as can be seen in Figure 2.

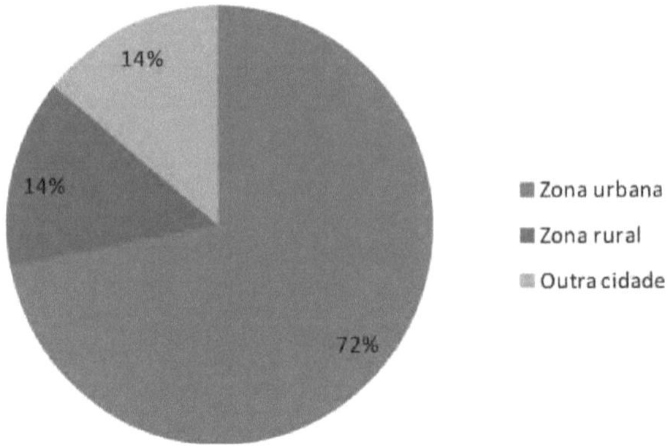

Figura 2: Graph of where distance learning students live

It's important to note that in order to attend higher education in an urban area, students from rural areas have to travel regularly, making it difficult for them to stay on the course, which is why the majority of the seven students who remain on the course, out of the 33 enrolled, are from urban areas.

Among those interviewed, 0% of the students are black. Those who consider themselves to be brown are the majority at 71%, while 29% consider themselves to be white, based on the understanding that the Brazilian black population is made up of "browns" and "blacks", as Osorio (2003) points out, which can be summed up as 71% black and 29% white.

Among the data published by Alcântara (2015), there is an equivalent distribution among the population of Grajau in terms of "color or race".

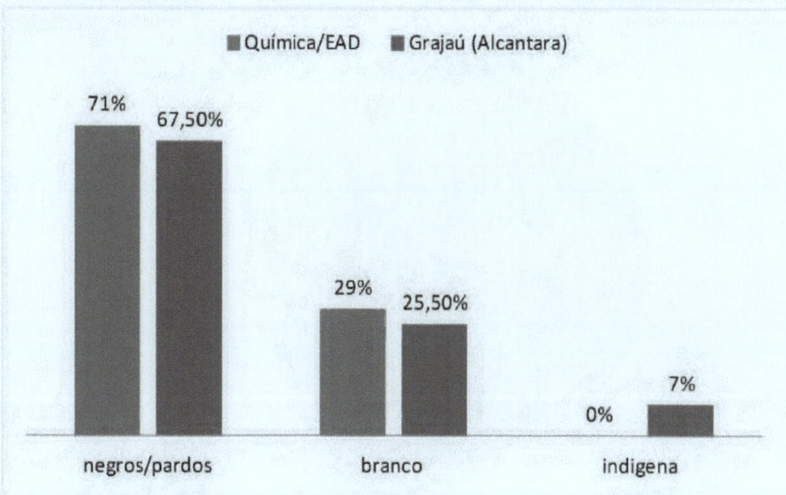

Figura 3: Comparison of the race/color of EAd Chemistry students with the population of Grajau according to Alcântara (2015).

In terms of schooling, 43% of the students already have a university degree in the classroom. Some students have degrees in teaching, such as Biological Sciences and Mathematics, and one student has a degree in nursing. According to Ferreira *et al.* (2007) professionals who seek out this type of education are generally interested in expanding their knowledge, improving their prospects of earning money and changing their professional training. The remaining students, 57%, do not have a university degree and are looking for a diploma to enter the job market, as can be seen in Figure 4.

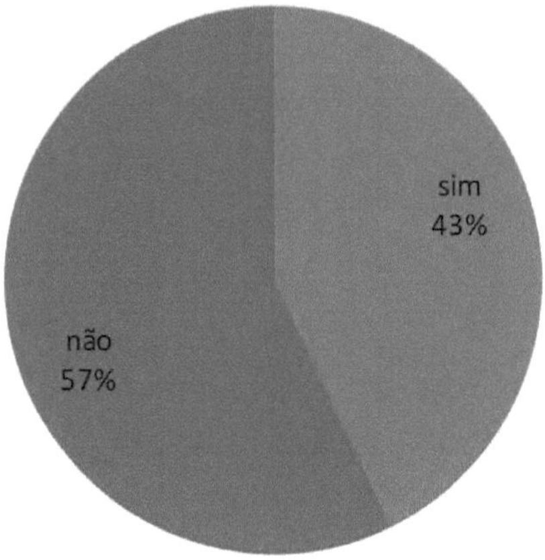

Figura 4: Graph of distance learning students' level of education

It was found that 29% of the students had already taken a distance learning course and 71% of those interviewed had never taken a distance learning course (Figure 5). According to Becker (2002), we must think of distance education in the same way as face-to-face education, we must think of the epistemology that underpins pedagogical work. In other words, teaching takes place within the limits of understanding how knowledge is constructed. We understand that we can't agree with teacher training that conceives of a passive student who only incorporates information that comes to them from outside.

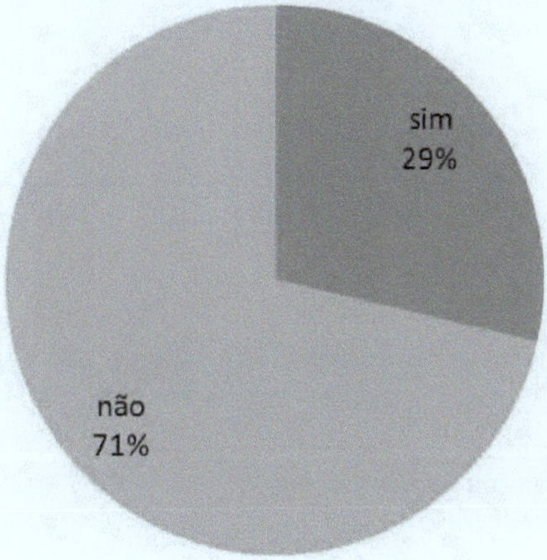

Figura 5: Graph on taking distance learning courses

Studying at home, whether in front of a computer or through books, should be taken seriously and with great responsibility. Many people choose distance learning because it best suits their professional and personal lives, mainly because of the busy schedules. But it's not just the time factor that has to be taken into account. Other points are also of fundamental importance in successfully completing the distance learning course, such as access to the internet, the lack of quality in the internet connection, not having the internet at home, the lack of the presence of both colleagues and teachers and time to study.

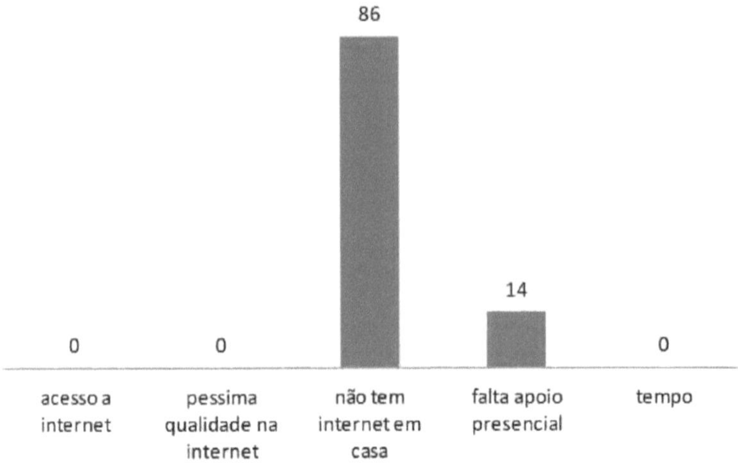

Figure 6: Graph on the main difficulty in distance learning

Figure 6 shows that 86% of those interviewed said that not having the internet at home was the main difficulty in distance learning, making it necessary to travel to the center to carry out activities. One student (14%) said that his biggest difficulty was the lack of face-to-face support, either from teachers at the center or the lack of interaction with colleagues to exchange experiences and difficulties.

This clear view that the internet would be the strength of distance education comes from the maturity of the students present at the hub (Figure 1), although many make it clear that the lack of face-to-face support is also an important factor. Many students are unable to study on their own without the presence of a face-to-face teacher. In distance learning, students need to break the paradigm that in order to learn they need the teacher in the classroom, where the presence of the teacher is not fundamental to the teaching-learning process, but rather the student's ability to be self-taught (Bittencourt and Mercado, 2014).

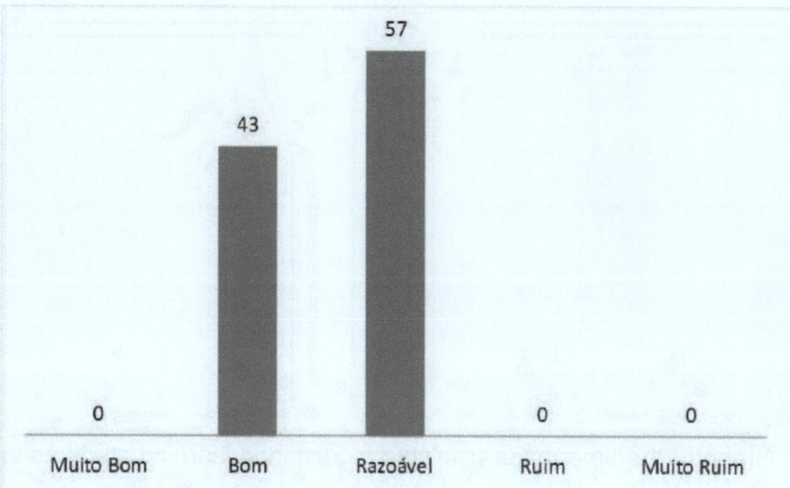

Figura 7: Students' knowledge of computers

The graph in Figure 7 shows that 43% of respondents rate their level of computer literacy as good and 57% of respondents consider their level of computer literacy to be reasonable.

Having good computer skills is contradictory to the reality and difficulties in

dealing with the virtual environment and using the tools used in distance education. According to Mercado (2007), among the difficulties in distance learning that cause frustration and abandonment is the insufficient technical mastery of ICT - especially the Internet. The inability to deal with ICT creates difficulties in keeping up with the activities proposed by distance learning courses, such as receiving and sending e-mails, participating in chats, discussion groups and visiting suggested links.

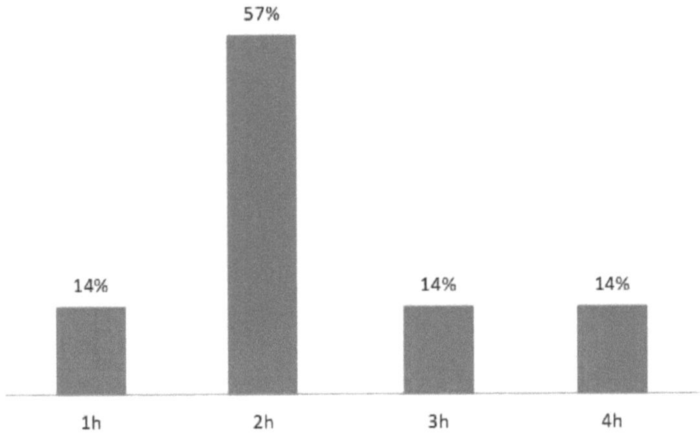

Figura 8: Graph of the time made available by distance learning students to carry out course activities.

With regard to the time available to distance learning students to carry out their course work, 14% of those interviewed made 1, 3 or 4 hours a day available to study and do their work. Of those interviewed, another 57% said that they spend 2 hours a day studying. That's an average of 2.26 hours a day for the course.

Of those interviewed, 28% said that distance education can be of the same quality as face-to-face education in the teaching of chemistry, because the difference is the students' attitude and interest in learning; students who study do well in any modality. 72% of those interviewed said no, because there are big differences and the lack of quality internet is the main difficulty faced by students at the Grajaù hub.

For Thompson (1996), research into distance education has emphasized that it is just as good a means of teaching as face-to-face education, or in some cases, due to the flexibility and interactivity of the new educational technologies, it can be superior, considering some specific situations and objectives, especially in the field of adult education. It can also mean an end to the geographical, economic, social, cultural and psychological distances that are often the main barriers to access to continuing training for teachers.

The students believe that they perform well in their activities in the following categories: autonomy in their studies; interactivity in the virtual environment; frequency of use of the virtual environment; digital content; technologies and pedagogical innovations of the course, showing a good performance in these which are essential for the smooth running of the course.

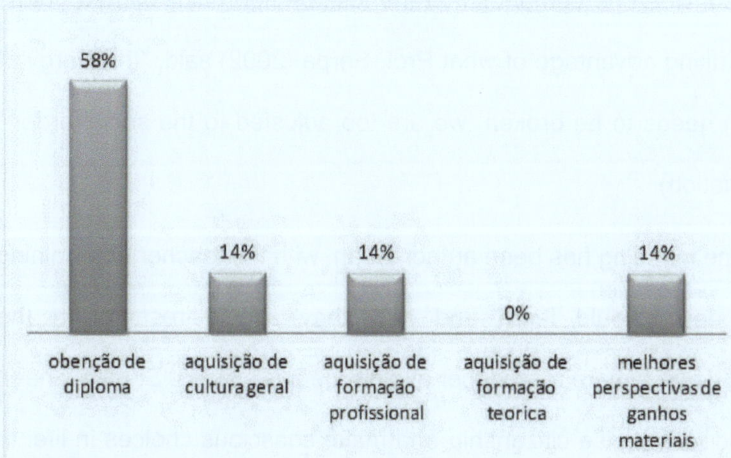

Figura 9: Acquisition of general culture, better prospects of material gain and the acquisition of professional training.

We could list several advantages of autonomous learning, but we'll mention a few according to CARVALHO (1994): it allows students to learn better and to seek greater depth in the subjects that interest them, since the teacher, faced with institutional curricular requirements and the time available, develops content that is considered essential, not allowing him or her the conditions to meet the students' options; it contributes to enriching the students' knowledge. We can see this, for example, when the teacher respects the different opinions of the students on the same subject; the students learn to free themselves from dependence on the teacher and begin to discover alternative ways of constructing knowledge.

What can be seen in the student's dependence on the teacher's guidance is part of the power game in the classroom and, most of the time, it is fed by the teacher himself, when he demands that the task be rigorously carried out as determined. Taking advantage of what Prof. Serpa (2002) said, "the liturgy of the classroom needs to be broken, we are too adjusted to the social order." (Verbal information).

Most of the time teaching has been authoritarian, with the teacher determining what the student should learn and how they should respond in the assessments, being a mere reproducer of other people's ideas. Students need to be prepared to exercise citizenship and make conscious choices in life. In distance learning, teachers need to realize the potential of this type of teaching without drawing parallels with classroom teaching.

What can be seen is the degree of dependence of students, due to the model they have received at home, in their social environment and even in educational institutions where they are given few opportunities to decide, making the individual dependent and with marked characteristics of mere reproducers, and in distance learning this needs to be rethought and immediately changed.

Even though it is a distance learning course, the student still needs face-to-face support, as the interviewee reports

"more video lessons, more face-to-face moments and, above all, more interaction between teacher and student (Interviewee 1)"

Knowledge of the tool is essential for both the teacher and the student, facilitating and offering greater learning possibilities.

It is important that the teacher knows the tools provided by the virtual environment and exploits them in a way that ensures that the student carries out different types of activities and develops different skills (interviewee 2).

The interviewees commented on the alternatives in distance education that would help them learn chemistry:

Interviewee 1 - More face-to-face classes and more support from the face-to-face tutor.

Interviewee 2 - Unfortunately, some of the technological tools didn't work as well as they should have, such as chats, video classes and videoconferences.

Don't you have interviewee 3?

Interviewee 5 - greater connectivity between students and teachers, a better internet connection would increase the possibility of video classes;

Interviewee 6 - More face-to-face classes and for the technological tools to work better, since most of our studies are done through these tools.

Interviewee 7 - That there should be more face-to-face moments, because being a course with a lot of calculations and formulas, you need to hear more explanations.

The questionnaire allowed some students to detail their opinion of the distance learning Chemistry course and they show satisfaction in acquiring great experience and knowledge with the course, as shown by the comment of interviewee 2, but they are very dissatisfied with the tools used, making it clear that they need to be improved.

I really enjoyed the course, because I learned a lot. I had several wonderful teachers, others not so much. There were several problems, including the technology not working well (Interviewee 2).

It can be seen from the interviewees' statements that, in general, despite some flaws in the distance learning process, the courses made available through this modality serve to remedy various problems of access to courses, especially with regard to the chemistry course, which is so badly needed in our schools due to the lack of teachers trained in this area.

6 conclusion

The analysis we made of the data obtained in the questionnaire leads us to believe that the students who sought out the degree course in Chemistry at the Federal University of Maranhao, in the distance modality, are between 30 and 40 years old, well divided between students with experience in other higher education courses and few already familiar with distance learning courses.

Although many were proficient in computers, they showed difficulties with the virtual environment and the lack of internet at home was the biggest difficulty in distance learning.

The answers given by some students also worry us about the lack of clarity about what distance education is and what it represents in terms of study autonomy. Many students, when reporting alternatives in distance education that would help them learn chemistry, emphasize more face-to-face moments.

Despite the not-so-elaborate imagery of distance learning and the lack of contact some of them have with communication and information technologies, this course will certainly make a difference for some of them and that is the meaning of university extension: we produce knowledge that places the institution among the best in the country. But this knowledge doesn't change the quality of life of the people who live further away from it, who don't even know about this production. We have no doubt that, by leaving its main "campus" and moving across the state through hubs, it will give people who are visibly excluded the opportunity to have access to a higher education course, even if this is a challenge beyond their expectations.

It's important to include a few observations you've made based on your results, as this way it becomes very general.

BIBLIOGRAPHICAL REFERENCES

Alcântara, R. L. S.; DIVERSITY AND COLONIALITY IN GRAJAÙ-MA: Challenges for teacher training. Inter Espaço Grajaù/MA v. 1, n. 1 p. 108-125; jan./jun.2015.

ANDRADE, Maria Margarida de. Introduçâo à metodologia do trabalho cientifico. 5. ed. Sâo Paulo: Atlas, 2001.

BECKER, F. and MARQUES, T.B.I. Ensino ou aprendizagem a distância. *Educar, Curitiba*, n° 19, 9. 85-98, 2002.

BELLONI, M.L. *Educaçâo a distância mais aprendizagem aberta.* Caxambu, 21ª Reuniâo Anual da ANPEd, GT Educaçâo e Comunicaçâo, 1998.

BELLONI, Maria Luiza. Distance Education. 4.ed.Sâo Paulo: Autores associados, 2006.

Bittencourt, I. M. and Mercado, L. P. L.; Evasion in distance education courses: a case study of the UFAL/UAB Administration Pilot Course. Ensaio: aval. pol. pùbl. Educ., Rio de Janeiro, v.22, n. 83, p. 465504, apr./jun. 2014

CARVALHO, lêda Matos Freire. Autonomous Learning, Genetic Epistemology and Pedagogical Practice. Unpublished article, 1994.

CensoEAD.BR - 2014/2015. Available at: http://www.abed.org.br/censoead2014/CensoEAD2014_portugues.pdf. accessed on March 10, 2016

Ferreira, Z. N.; Mendonça, G. A. A. Mendonça, A. F. O perfil do aluno de educaçâo a distância no ambiente TELEDUC. Research Report, CEFET- GO, 2007.

JAPIASSU, Hilton. Preface. In: FAZENDA, Ivani Catarina Arantes (Org.) Integraçâo e interdisciplinaridade no ensino brasileiro: efetividade ou ideologia? Sâo Paulo: Loyola, 1983.

Lei de Diretrizes e Bases da Educaçâo Nacional Law No. 9.394, of December 20, 1996.

LEITE, L. S.; VIEIRA, M. L. S.; SAMPAIO, M. N. Non-face-to-face activities: preparing students for autonomy. **Tecnologia Educacional**, Rio de Janeiro, ABT, ano. 26, n.141, p.36-40, trimestral. 1997.

MARANHAO. Federal University of Maranhão (UFMA). **Pedagogical Project for the Undergraduate Chemistry Course**. Sâo Luis - MA, 2007, p. 9.

Mercado, L. P.L.; Difficulties in online distance education. April, 2007. Available at:

http://www.abed.org.br/congresso2007/tc/55200761718PM.pdf. accessed on March 13, 2016.

MINAS GERAIS. Federal University of Minas Gerais (UFMG). **Pedagogical Project for the Undergraduate Chemistry Course**. Belo Horizonte - MG, 2005, p. 9-10.

NAKAMURA, Rodolfo. **Moodle**: how to create a course using the Distance Learning platform. Sâo Paulo: Farol do Forte, 2009.

OSORIO, Rafael Guerreiro. The "color or race" classification system of the IBGE . Brasilia: IPEA, 2003

PALLOFF, Rena M.; PRATT, Keith. Building learning communities in cyberspace: effective strategies for the online classroom. Translation by Vinicius Figueira. Porto Alegre: Artmed, 2002.

PIMENTEL, N. M. O ensino a distância na formação de professores: relato da experiência do programa "Um salto para o futuro". **Perspectiva**, Florianópolis, n. 24, p. 93-128, jul./dez. 1995.

PALLOFF, Rena M; PRATT, Keith. The Virtual Learner: a guide to working with online students. Porto Alegre: Artmed, 2004.

RIBEIRO, Elvia Nunes; MENDONÇA, Gilda Aquino de Araùjo; MENDONÇA, Alzino Furtado de. The importance of virtual learning environments in the search for new domains of distance learning. 2007. p.4. Available at: Accessed on: October 16, 2015.

SABBATINI, Renato Marcos Endrizzi. Teaching and learning environment via the Internet: the Moodle Platform. Instituto EduMed, 2007. p.1. Available at: http://www.ead.edumed.org. br/file.php/1/PlataformaMoodle.pdf. Accessed on: October 16, 2015.

MUNNICIPAL EDUCATION SECRETARIAT - SEDUC - Grajaù-MA - 2014.

SOARES, Ismar de Oliveira. Collaborative work and new means of producing knowledge: an educommunicative proposal. Sâo Paulo, 2003. p.14. Available at: . Accessed on: October 19, 2015.

THOMPSON, M.M. Distance delivery of postgraduate teacher training: beyond parity claims. Revista Educaçâo Superior Continuada, v 44. (3), 29-34 pp., 1996.

UNIVERSIDADE ABERTA DO BRASIL (UAB) - Bairro Trizidela - Polo - Grajaù-MA.

VIGOTSKY, L. S. The social formation of the mind. Sâo Paulo: Martins Fontes, 1984.

www.ibge.gov.br/home/estatistica/populacao/.../pnad2006. Accessed on Oct 15, 2015

APPENDIX

QUESTIONNAIRE

1 How old are you?

( ) 18 to 20 ( ) 20 to 30 ( ) 30 to 40 ( ) 40 to 50 or more

2 Where do you live?

( ) Urban area ( ) Rural area ( ) Other city

3 What is your ethnicity/color?

( ) Black ( ) brown ( ) white ( ) indigenous

4 Do you already have another degree?

( ) yes ( ) no

5 Have you ever taken a distance learning course?

( ) yes ( ) no

6 What is the main difficulty in distance learning?

( ) Internet access

( ) Poor internet quality

( ) no internet at home

( ) Lack of face-to-face support

7 How would you rate your computer skills?

( ) Very good ( ) Good ( ) Fair ( ) Poor

8 How much time do you have per day to spend on course activities?

( )1h ( )2h ( )3h

9 Which strategy did you learn the most about?

( ) Chat ( ) Forum ( ) Video classes ( ) Face-to-face meetings ( ) Other

10 Can distance education have the same quality as face-to-face education in chemistry?

( ) yes ( ) no

11 What is the main contribution of the course?

( ) Obtaining a higher education diploma

( ) The acquisition of general culture

( ) The acquisition of professional training

( ) The acquisition of theoretical training

( ) Improved prospects for material gains

Score your performance in the following categories from 0 to 10

12 Automation in your studies ______________________________

13 Interactivity in the virtual environment ______________________

14 Frequency of use of the virtual environment _________________

15 Digital content ______________________________________

16 Technology ____

17 Pedagogical innovations in the course

MIX
Papier aus verantwortungsvollen Quellen
Paper from responsible sources
FSC® C105338

Printed by Books on Demand GmbH, Norderstedt / Germany